GLIMMERS

GLIMMERS

How to find pockets of joy in every day

HAYLEY DOYLE

PAVILION

CONTENTS

'How far that little candle throws
his beams!
So shines a good deed in
a naughty world.'

WILLIAM SHAKESPEARE
The Merchant of Venice

INTRODUCTION

I've always thought of myself as a cheap date. Classy, right?

It's not that I get hammered after half a cider or anything. I'm just all about the micro-moments. Those funny realizations or sparks of electricity; that mini 'Oh wow!' that can create a superb memory. I've been taken to fancy restaurants that felt rather soulless when the mood just didn't get off on the right foot. On the other hand, I subconsciously fell in love with my husband beside a pop-up stall selling bacon rolls at the rugby (and I'm definitely not into rugby).

A good pal once told me that I'm a glass-half-full kind of person. Do I go about my life with my head in the clouds chasing rainbows? Ha, I wish. Full disclaimer: I'm known to sulk, and I can get really annoyed with people just for being people. You'll easily catch me having a good ol' moan too. I'm always more than happy to chew the fat – let it all out, my friend!

But I also love life. I love it wholeheartedly. I go to bed late because I'm sad to bid farewell to the day we're in. There's so much to do. I just want to do everything! And by this, I mean the little things. The stuff that really makes me happy. Doing a 1,500-piece jigsaw while listening to the radio in the kitchen. Playing the piano – badly – but feeling that fizz of excitement when I hit the right notes, especially if I've managed to use both hands and multiple fingers.

I'm so glad I've come to this realization. I'm relieved. In the past, precious years – decades, even – were spent chasing ambition. I was convinced that all sorts of heartaches would be healed by major achievements and impressive accolades. If you'd asked me as a child what would've made me happy when I grew up, I would've probably said something along the lines of being a Hollywood movie star. Okay, I still watch the Oscars and like to fantasize about what it'd be like to dress (or be dressed) for the red carpet. We've all rehearsed our winner's speech in the bathroom mirror holding a shampoo bottle, right? But when I think back over the highlights of my career – the bucket-list ticks and the big goals scored – in truth, I feel conflicted. Reality is so often peppered with disillusionment. Expectations rarely met. Questions left unanswered.

Once upon a time, it was my dream to make it on the West End stage. This dream came true when I was 24 years old. While it carved out a path for me to follow and was in many ways a defining point in my life and career, it was also the mid-noughties, and a higher tolerance for bullying in the workplace brought its fair share of pain, which can still pinch to this day. The sweetest memories I have of that time are the small pockets of joy: the sisterhood in our dressing room, the warmth of the stage lights on my face and, strangely, the biscuity smell of fake tan. Happiness doesn't linger in the main event, it pops up in beautiful little bubbles.

'I LIKE TO LET THAT HUGE, WIDE WORLD OUT THERE KNOW THAT THE SMALL THINGS REALLY CAN MATTER.'

Those who know me will vouch for me being the person who bites into a burger and announces to the whole table how damn good it tastes. I'm a sucker for a scenic view – seriously, get me in the passenger seat as we drive across a bridge and you'll witness me transform into a kid on Christmas morning. And don't get me started on Christmas. I am Kevin McCallister's kindred spirit with my deep love of Christmas trees. I've seen so many in my life, yet they never fail to lighten my spirit. Even the tacky tinsel ones.

To spell it out for you, if there's something bothering me, you'll know about it. But if something gives me joy, I embrace it with my heart and soul. I say it out loud. I like to let that huge, wide world out there know that the small things really can matter. Buttered toast. April blossoms on the trees by my local train station. My furry hot-water bottle. A neon sunset. Chocolate, cold and hard from being kept in the fridge. The satisfying fit of my children's hands in mine when we cross the road. A crescent moon in a clear night sky. Child's pose. Lemongrass. Reaching the final page of a book. A key change, especially in a show tune. Getting a ride on a golf buggy. Chippy chips...

The list goes on. Some people might roll their eyes and think, 'Ugh, she's always so chirpy'. It's not that my life is without hurt, worry or struggle. I just enjoy what I enjoy, and I'm becoming increasingly aware that what I enjoy doesn't have to be too grand or out of reach. I still get scared that I won't achieve my goals, and anxious about the passing of time. Overwhelm occurs often – being a parent, being a woman, being human. But I do smile a lot and I share my feelings. I believe that seeing the beauty in micro-moments is what makes me a happy person. Yes, there's trauma to be dealt with, and I am forever learning about my triggers. But just as *yin* needs *yang* and eggs need bacon, triggers need ... *glimmers*.

A DAY IN THE
✦ LIFE OF...

What can a daily glimmer look like?

The term 'glimmers' was coined by trauma specialist Deb Dana, who used it in her 2018 book *Polyvagal Theory in Therapy* to describe the opposite of a trigger. I'll discuss that in greater detail on page 21, but for now, all you need to know is that glimmers are unpredictable, and they are happening all around us.

Let's imagine a cold and dark Tuesday morning in London. Sam steps out of the shower shivering as he grabs his towel off the piping-hot radiator. Wrapping it around his body, he sighs with deep satisfaction, feeling it embrace him like a warm hug. For a micro-moment, he feels at one with the world.

Next door, Vivi pours fresh coffee into her favourite mug: sunflower yellow and decorated with a golden V. She holds it with both hands close to her chin. Leaning against her kitchen table she inhales. Her lips touch the aromatic liquid. Damn, that feels good.

A short while later, on the London Underground, Lola arrives on the platform just as her train pulls in. As the doors slide open, she hops aboard and spots an empty seat. 'Today is a good day,' she thinks.

Kim is on the same train. Pregnant – but not yet showing – she feels nauseous, but she's not comfortable about asking for a seat. She grabs the rail tightly as more passengers board, crowding her space. Finally she gets to her stop and exits, through the station and out down a quiet city street. She feels a gentle breeze as the bright morning sun tickles her cheeks. She smiles. This fleeting moment feels personal – as if nature wants to hold her safe in its arms.

Meanwhile, Ash has decided to work from home. He's suffering from a lingering cold and he has a pile of admin to get through. As he opens his laptop, he glances outside, distracted by the dark turn in the weather. Rain begins to fall, splattering against the window. As he sits watching the dance of the water on the glass, and its increasing intensity, he realizes what a great decision it was to stay home. He releases a long, contented sigh before getting up to make a cup of tea.

Elsewhere, as lunchtime arrives, Jay cooks a boiled egg. His knife slices the egg in two and a bright orange gooey yolk spills onto his slice of sourdough like poster paint. Thick, satisfying and perfect for dipping, he thinks.

In a backyard across town, Alex strokes his neighbour's cat, Misty, savouring the silky feel of her fur. Misty purrs.

After a meeting in a central office, when his boss is out of earshot, Lou cracks a joke stolen from his favourite character in an old episode of *Only Fools and Horses*. It sums up the situation perfectly and really tickles the rest of team, who then begin sharing impressions of their own from the show.

On her walk home from school, Nina spots not one but two ladybirds crawling across a wall. She watches them scurry along, while her mum chats with another parent. Whatever it is that they're talking about, they agree with each other.

They nod their heads, exchange a hug. Then Nina hears her mum say, 'Thank you'. 'Anytime,' the other mum replies.

Ben is listening to the radio while hanging out his laundry. His favourite song from his student days comes on. He starts to play air guitar and closes his eyes as he sings the bridge, using a clean sock as a microphone.

Anna stops tidying when she comes across an old photo album under her bed. She opens it and, seeing the haphazardly arranged and slightly blurry photos, a bittersweet memory makes her heart swell. Shoulder pads, perms, shell suits and ... her first crush.

After being stuck in traffic for an hour, Nicky opens their front door and is hit with a delicious waft of sizzling bacon coming from the kitchen.

When Finn crawls into bed that night, he inhales the freshly washed sheets and snuggles into their crisp cleanliness.

Maryam has worked the late shift. She pulls into her driveway, gets out of her car and tilts her head to alleviate a crick in her neck. She looks up at the stars; there's the Plough (aka Big Dipper). Like bold silver buttons. She then spots even more stars freckling the navy sky, awed by the overwhelming vastness of the universe.

Glimmers really are everywhere. From morning until night, from the mundane to the awesome. And everybody is capable of experiencing them.

Are you ready to recognize the extraordinary in the ordinary?

'It has always seemed to me, ever since early childhood, that, amid all the commonplaces of life, I was very near to a kingdom of ideal beauty. Between it and me hung only a thin veil. I could never draw it quite aside, but sometimes a wind fluttered it and I caught a glimpse of the enchanting realm beyond— only a glimpse – but those glimpses have always made life worth while.'

LUCY MAUD MONTGOMERY
The Alpine Path

FINDING ✦ WONDER IN THE ✦ ORDINARY

A glimmer is a small moment of joy. It can happen anytime, anywhere.

You just have to notice it. Easy, right?

Not quite.

Glimmers can often slip past without us appreciating them. We're human. And this means we're born with a negative bias. Our minds naturally sway this way to protect us from being blindsided by disappointment or worse. The news is bad, so what do we do? We devour it. There's a traffic incident, so how do we react? We drive past slowly to nose at the impact. Our boss is heading towards our desk, so what do we think? Oops, we're in trouble. We can thank the good old prehistoric days for this. Back then, the only way to increase the likelihood of survival was by sniffing out every potential threat in sight. Individuals on red alert for danger managed to stay alive longer and we've inherited this defence mechanism. Our instincts tell us that it protects us.

Humans also have a natural drive for self-improvement. We're obsessed with progress. As children, we're told to make wishes as we blow out the candles on our birthday cake. As we get older, the desire for our wishes to come true doesn't leave us, it's just that those wishes transition from wanting a pet unicorn to wanting a loft extension. 'One day, when I'm rich and famous,' we say. Or we fantasize about winning the lottery or meeting the love of our life. This need to enhance our lot is innate, whether it's personal growth, career advancement or material comfort.

But a wish – or more simply, a need – is a bit like the internet. Never-ending. You might find exactly what you were looking for, but you'll easily be enticed down a path seeking something beyond your original goal. Just as one need is met, there's another waiting in the wings. And another. And another. And once basic needs like food and shelter are met, higher-level needs kick in.

Again, this is how we have evolved. Humans progressed in group settings where cooperation and communication were essential for survival. Today, we are quick to pick up on social cues and highly influenced by the actions and opinions of others. Seeing somebody cry – even if the reason is unclear – can make another person well up, while coming home to see your next-door neighbour's brand new BMW parked on their driveway can spark a pang of desire to own something similar (or better). Although humans are conformists, desperate to be accepted among our peers, we're also driven by curiosity. Just ask Alice – she had one hell of a ride trying to find out where the white rabbit was going and why he was so late. Exploring new possibilities and exciting experiences give us the satisfaction of self-improvement, but what happens after the thrill of the rollercoaster? Well, you want to go on an even bigger one.

'EACH GLIMMER YOU FIND BELONGS TO YOU – IT'S WHATEVER FILLS YOUR CUP OF JOY IN THAT PARTICULAR MOMENT.'

It seems we're never happy. If one wish comes true, another wish soon arises. Like praying to your god of choice every night for that big job, only to land the opportunity and soon finding yourself back on your knees praying for a change in career. Or longing for love, until it serenades you with a cringey red rose. Date nights turn into binge-watching and you catch yourself thinking, 'I wish I was single again'. Reality always comes a-knocking. We can't spend all our days craving what we don't have. It's back to work, back to the grind. Our dreams are put on hold and then, watch out – we're back in the cave again, thinking the worst.

The problem with having a basket full of wishes is the anticlimax that comes when a magic wand fails to wave. We question our abilities or our decisions. We might want to slam a door and indulge in sulky solitude. While occasional disappointment is a normal part of the human experience, living with a dispirited heaviness can trigger physiological responses similar to those of stress, such as an increased heart rate, elevated blood pressure and changes in hormone levels. As Dr Richard Boyatzis, Professor of Organizational Behaviour, Psychology and Cognitive Science at Ohio's Case Western Reserve University, has pointed out, 'You need the negative focus to survive … but a positive one to thrive.'

In short, what you need are glimmers.

Glimmers are rooted in what's known as 'polyvagal theory' – put simply, the way that the nervous system impacts mental health. The vagus nerve is the longest nerve in our autonomic nervous system and it plays a significant role in regulating various bodily functions, including heart rate, digestion and mood. Research has shown that the vagus nerve is involved in the body's stress response and relaxation mechanisms. When activated, it can promote relaxation and reduce the physiological signs of stress, lowering the heart rate and blood pressure. Techniques that stimulate the vagus nerve, such as deep breathing, meditation and yoga, are therefore associated with improved wellbeing.

Deb Dana, the author who coined the term 'glimmers', is a clinical social worker who specializes in complex trauma. As she explains, 'Glimmers refer to small moments when our biology is in a place of connection or regulation, which cues our nervous system to feel safe or calm.' Whereas triggers are cues that prompt fight-or-flight states, glimmers are cues that push the opposite buttons; they prompt feelings of safety and connection. Activating the vagus nerve is often involuntary – for example, if you're stressed or anxious. But it is possible to regulate this yourself and to stimulate the vagus nerve. Breathing deeply can reduce a fight-or-flight state, and although the vagus nerve kicks into action when trauma is experienced, it can also help create positive memories, and assist in coping with traumatic flashbacks or intrusive thoughts.

A ping of insight, a spark of realization, something that makes you catch your breath – these are all glimmers. But since they don't stick around for very long, how can they have a positive effect on mental health? It's all very well getting a whiff of aftershave that reminds you of somebody you love, but it doesn't turn the clock back if you're rushing to get to work on time. It may be lovely to roll your cheek onto that blissfully cool patch of untouched pillow in the morning, but you still have to get up when the alarm goes off. What if all these moments of pure pleasure result in us falling back down to earth with a hard thud each time?

When it comes to the power of glimmers, Deb explains, 'We're not talking great, big, expansive experiences of joy or safety or connection, these are micro-moments that begin to shape our system in very gentle ways.'

Let's pretend it's your wedding day. The Best Day of Your Life. Attention to detail has left no stone – or diamanté – unturned. You've noted the dietary requirements for every single guest, Uncle Bob has been seated at a safe distance from Auntie Val, and you've even spent half of your savings getting the First Dance choreographed by a *Strictly* pro, but hey, it's gonna be so worth it. Each tiny element has had so much thought poured into it that you and your partner have a permanent headache, but it's fine because it's guaranteed to be the Best Day Ever. What could go possibly wrong?

Eek. Well, the stakes are super high for a start. You might have sampled ten different textures of cake in advance to hit the tier-tastic jackpot, but you can't digest this level of stress and anxiety. Of course it's a joy to see all of your favourite faces in one room, but this might be overshadowed by social obligations and performance expectations, with the pressure of everybody fancying a piece of you (followed by a dollop of guilt if you can't come up with the goods). On top of that, there's a traffic jam. And an electrical fault that makes the festoon lights flicker. And that friend who gets totally wasted and projectile-vomits on your mum's fascinator. Predictably, your negativity bias comes galloping in on horseback when the sun gets shielded by clouds because of course – OF COURSE – it starts to rain.

Where's the intimacy? Where's the joy?

'IMMERSING
YOURSELF
IN THE PRESENT
MOMENT CAN
TURN THE
VOLUME DOWN
ON THE NOISE
AROUND YOU.'

It's all there. In the small moments. Despite this hypothetical wedding being a rather clichéd disaster, there will have been oodles of glimmers along the way. The hairdresser holding up a mirror to show you the finished result. The one-liner your pal came out with while waiting for the cars to arrive. That classic eighties tune on the radio en route. The warm breeze that settled your nerves before the ceremony. The smile radiating from your partner as they caught your eye.

Small moments allow for spontaneity and relaxation. If each moment is a building block, they can stack up to create a tower of happiness. Small moments come with fewer expectations, too, and in return they can create opportunities for mindfulness. Immersing yourself in the present moment can turn the volume down on the noise around you, creating space – space to breathe, space to think, space to be.

Big events with rigid schedules and formalities can feel claustrophobic. It can become more of a pressure than a joy to make memories. But honing in on the intricacies of the day will create the flexibility and freedom you need to feel fulfilled. Now, I'm not suggesting you steer clear of the big fat wedding, if that's what your heart desires. But I am encouraging you to look out for the glimmers that could elevate your day. If things go wrong – or, when things go wrong, because they invariably do – the blow will be softened if your mind is in tune with the many micro-positives.

This can all sound a little airy-fairy, I know. A bit like skipping around in a meadow all day long, chasing butterflies and sniffing freshly cut grass. But it's worth being aware of the fact that we naturally tend to curse our misfortunes. I bet if I asked what triggers you, you'd reel off a list without hesitation. We are so primed to be triggered, and encouraged to know what our triggers are. How else are we supposed to avoid them? Face them? Fight them? But let's flip this around for a minute and imagine being encouraged to recognize our glimmers instead. Yours might be very different to the next person's. Each glimmer you find belongs to you – it's whatever fills your cup of joy in that particular moment.

A small shift in mindset is all it takes; mini-adjustments rather than massive lifestyle changes. It doesn't require deep meditation. There's no need to sign up for an online course. You don't even have to leave the comfort of your own bed (a glimmer). You know when you're sitting in an awkward position, on the verge of pins and needles, yet you just can't be bothered to move? Then you bite the bullet, move and … aah, that feels better.

Hello glimmer.

'A SMALL SHIFT
IN MINDSET
IS ALL IT
TAKES; MINI-
ADJUSTMENTS
RATHER THAN
MASSIVE
LIFESTYLE
CHANGES.'

DID YOU KNOW THAT GLIMMERS CAN...

Enhance self-awareness
Acknowledging – and reflecting on – moments of insight can make us more attuned to our thoughts and feelings, and how we behave daily.

Encourage learning and growth
Placing value upon moments of realization can allow you to become more open to new ideas and fresh perspectives.

Improve problem-solving skills
Glimmers often occur when we approach problems from fresh angles. It's a wonderful feeling to connect the dots! Paying close attention to these satisfying moments can foster creativity and innovation.

Boost confidence

Experiencing a glimmer can be empowering. It confirms your ability to understand complex concepts, solve problems and find joy. You then begin to appreciate who you really are at your core.

Reduce stress

Glimmers are often accompanied by a sense of clarity and understanding. You can breathe, relax. These moments can promote emotional wellbeing and build resilience for dealing with everyday stressors.

Foster connection

By discussing your glimmers with other people, you can learn from each other. The conversation is positive from all angles. By collaborating over ideas, you are forging relationships.

Because glimmers exist within a light, fleeting moment, it can be difficult to take them seriously. Try and give them the credit they deserve, though, because a glimmer ain't just a pretty flower.

'GLIMMERS ARE
NOT ABOUT
TRYING TO SEE
THE GOOD IN
EVERYTHING –
THEY'RE ABOUT
NOTICING *WHEN*
SOMETHING
IS GOOD.'

GLIMMERS VS TOXIC ✦ ✦ POSITIVITY

Glimmers are not part of the 'toxic positivity' world...

| 'Cheer up!'

'You were too good for him anyway!' |

| 'Look, things could be worse!'

'You're lucky to be alive!' |

Toxic positivity whitewashes all the bad stuff and pretends that everything is good. This destructive phenomenon is simply maintaining the relentless illusion of being happy. It stifles genuine human connections, destroys self-esteem, and undermines workplace and popular culture.

It also leaves you in a constant state of uncertainty. Toxic positivity forces you to write a narrative to your life that might be untrue. With a glimmer, however, you're not gaslighting yourself. Nobody's trying to sell you anything. You're in your truest state and loving exactly what you love. It's like sliding your feet into your slippers at the end of a long day.

Toxic positivity creates the pressure to be unrealistically optimistic without considering the true circumstances of a situation, forcing you to put on a brave or happy face regardless. Glimmers do not mute the struggles we face; they simply make the difficult parts a bit easier to manage.

Glimmers are not about trying to see the good in everything – they're about noticing *when* something is good. Like when you bite into a brownie and taste the salted caramel; acknowledging that a moment can provide deep satisfaction, even if it only lasts for a couple of seconds. And glimmers can occur in any given moment, good *or* bad: your career might be in the toilet, but your heart can still smile at the sight of a beautiful piece of art.

WHERE DO ✦ ✦ I START?

Let's face it, you've likely had a couple of negative thoughts today already.

If I hear a dog barking, for example, I am transported in a flash to being a toddler, when a yapping terrier bit my face and I was rushed to hospital in a neighbour's car. My heart rate speeds up and it can take a while to regulate my breathing again. This trigger is a mental note written in permanent marker, lodged in my brain. Luckily, glimmers are penned in permanent marker, too ... and in the colour of your choice!

Before you rush off to the stationery shop or fill your online basket with pens and Post-its, close your eyes, take three deep breaths, then try one of these simple visualization exercises to set your inner glimmers aglow:

Picture yourself in your happy place and don't worry if you've never been there! It can be inspired by a photo or a movie, any tranquil spot of beauty created in your imagination, or a place you've been to and absolutely love. The important thing is that it's somewhere you desire to be.

Who – or what – has ever made you feel safe? This can be a wish or a memory. Think of anything that you associate with feelings of warmth, like when someone special hugs you or the smell of a home-cooked meal.

Revisit your childhood, which might mean a soft toy you loved, fish fingers and spaghetti hoops (SpaghettiOs), playing outside until the street lamps came on and signalled that it was time to go home. If you'd rather not recall early memories, think about what comforts you now, or what you think might unlock that childlike joy.

Think about a loved one, and this means anybody you feel relaxed around; somebody you're able to just be yourself with. Think about giving them a quick call and arranging to spend some time together. Or if this isn't possible, plan to listen to a song that reminds you of time spent together.

Now open your eyes and scribble down anything that comes to mind: words, phrases, colours, textures, lyrics, names. Allow the writing to be as abstract and jumbled up as you like. Make a list, then underline your favourite elements or circle them with bright colours.

'YOUR
HAPPY PLACE
CAN BE ANY
TRANQUIL SPOT
OF BEAUTY
CREATED
IN YOUR
IMAGINATION.'

Make a glimmer-gram!

This exercise consists of drawing a series of circles, with the biggest one roughly in the centre. In that circle, insert an object, memory or person that makes you happy, then see where this leads to. This example comes from Gemma, 42, a teacher from Nottingham, UK. Let the example on this page inspire you into action on the following pages.

My dad's hugs

Listening to Elton John LPs with my dad and my brother

The old record player with built-in cassette player in our old house

That dance we made up to 'Crocodile Rock'

My besties – it's a miracle we could get together for this

When Kelly fell into the pool at Debbie's hen do

They've always got my back

Too many ridiculous in-jokes

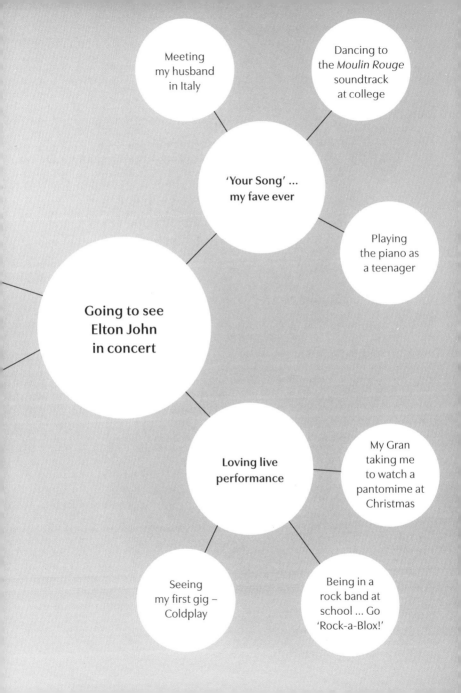

Your turn!

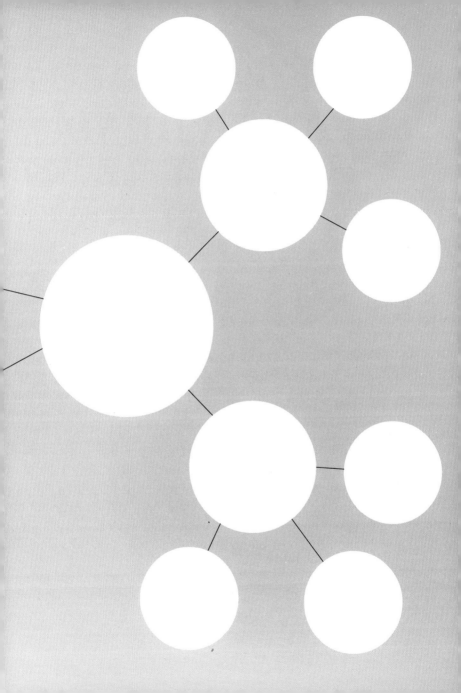

OFF THE TOP
OF YOUR HEAD
part 1

Some glimmers are utterly personal. They occur when you're on your own. Licking uncooked cake mix off a wooden spoon or hearing birds chirping on a sunny day – whatever lands well within your nervous system is what determines a moment that's meant just for you.

Other glimmers might be shared with another living being: when a cat curls up on your lap and purrs, when you belly-laugh with a friend, when a stranger connects with you for a brief moment.

Write down three glimmers that spring to mind.

What simple things make you happy? Be as universal or as abstract as you wish. Don't overthink it either – you can always make a longer list later (see page 148). For now, just see what falls naturally from pen to paper...

1.
....

2.
....

3.
....

Make a habit of chatting to your friends, family and colleagues about glimmers. You'll find that it's contagious. Once you open up a conversation about little pockets of joy, others will join the line like a conga at a kids' disco. Sort of like this...

'I love that feeling of lying in Shavasana at the end of a yoga class.'

'Hmm, I'm not into yoga but I get such a buzz when I finish a run.'

'When I run, I listen to music, and sometimes a cool breeze hits me as the intro of one of my favourite songs kicks in, it's so amazing.'

'Ha, I'll tell you what's amazing – an empty inbox!'

'Or the first page of a brand new notebook...'

'...writing a to-do list and crossing each item off with a really smooth gel pen!'

'Gel pens in general. They're so satisfying to write with.'

'The satisfaction of bedtime, done. I mean, I love my kids, but I also really love it when they're asleep. I watch their chests rise and fall, and listen to their breath. I kiss their warm bubble cheeks.'

'Adorable ... like smelling your baby's head!'

'It doesn't have to be my baby. Any baby!'

'I wouldn't say babies feature in a glimmer to me ... but Ryan Gosling would!'

'What would Ryan Gosling have to do to be a glimmer?'

'Ugh, just his voice alone sends me into a fizz.'

'The voice of someone you love! That's a good glimmer.'

'The sound of a champagne cork popping...'

'...and that first sip when you feel the bubbles tickling your nostrils!'

'Honestly, I just love to sit back in my chair and rub my baldy head.'

'Nice! And I love to stick my finger into a new jar of peanut butter...'

'...what about an already-opened jar?'

'Sure, I'll take that over an empty jar any day!'

If you're now starting to think of more glimmers, expand the list you started. Jot them down in a journal or write them on Post-it notes. Your nervous system is starting to reap some juicy rewards as you become more present, aware and engaged.

Send yourself a voice note. Tell a friend. Spread the joy!

'PAUSE WITHIN THAT GLIMMER. ALLOW IT TO PERMEATE FOR EVEN LONGER, TAKING THAT SUNBEAM DEEP INSIDE OF YOU.'

BECOMING ✦ THE GLIMMER

'You have the power within you.' – Linda Steiner

'Glimmers – wonderful, wonderful things,' says Linda Steiner, a UK-based psychoanalytic psychotherapist specializing in child, adolescent and family psychotherapy. 'To me, they really are the *stuff* of life. They have the capacity to completely light us up.'

A glimmer doesn't need to be physical – something you can see, touch or hold – it can also be metaphorical. As Linda Steiner explains, 'When you see a ray of sun breaking through the clouds, if you look closely and allow yourself to feel it, you can *become* that ray of light. Your mood can mirror the sunbeam.' Whether or not you're inclined to believe in magic, embodying a glimmer – *becoming* the glimmer – is rather magical.

The glimmers offered by nature evoke largeness and growth, connecting us with the world. They simply make us feel good. The smell of the sea and its salty air, hand in hand with the sound of the waves lapping against the shore, can take us to a big, big place – the enormity of the ocean and its wonders. 'We're reminded in the most beautiful sense how we're only here for a short time,' Linda explains. 'How we have this opportunity to be a part of this enormous universe, full of stars, moons, and planets.'

For those of us who are more introspective, Linda is careful to add that, however deep that introspection goes, it's always worth thinking about glimmers. 'Try to open your mind and your heart to them. Connect to what is around you. You don't need to be a therapist to find glimmers, or have a therapist to find them. You don't need medication to get a glimmer into your life. They're free. And they're all around us.'

Linda stresses the importance of noticing these everyday magical moments for mental health and wellbeing. 'Some of us notice them more than others. If you're the sort of person who happens to naturally recognize the small things that bring you that little bit of joy, that's a fantastic sign. It means you're there, living your life with a positive outlook. You have the ability to hone in on what's around you.' And it doesn't have to end there. If you're attuned to spotting glimmers, keep going. 'Pause within that glimmer. Allow it to permeate for even longer, taking that sunbeam deep inside of you. Own it. Such a moment of stillness and appreciation can be incredibly powerful.'

Glimmers can be so many things. They can evoke any of our senses. Linda enjoys the aroma of coconut tanning oil because she associates it with a memorable holiday many years ago. 'I only have to get a small waft of it and I'm there. I'm back on that beach. I can almost hear the banging club tunes in the background! It's like I've had a quick free holiday, for a little glimmer of time.'

It's likely happened to all of us. We walk past a stranger, get a whiff of their perfume and it sparks a reminder of somebody you hold dear; the smell allows you to revisit them in the moment.

Not everybody is able to find glimmers easily, though. Linda's advice is to try and educate ourselves – to understand that we can all learn to spot them with the smallest of steps. 'Initially, it might be simply trying to notice the sun coming through the clouds. This is enough. Stop there. You can work on those sunbeams getting bigger.'

REVISITING
+ THE +
MOMENT

A childhood memory can be the gateway to a lifelong glimmer.

Every week, I take my kids to swimming lessons and I'm telling you – there's not a glimmer in sight in those changing rooms! It's like aliens have invaded the adults' bodies, leaving them without spatial awareness or simple communication skills. I can forgive a shivering child who can't walk in a straight line to the showers, but a fully grown adult? And when it comes to afterschool activities, nothing is more oversubscribed than swimming. So, yeah, Tuesdays around 4 pm are right up there on a list of things I'd rather not be doing. Like walking on hot coals, or running a marathon. However, there *is* always a glimmer, and this comes in the form of a memory – thanks to the smell of chlorine...

There's a distinct smell when you walk into a sports centre with an indoor pool. It's usually partnered with a specific sound, too – a thick echo of children squealing and splashing. Every time my senses picks up that chlorine smell and those hazy sounds, a smile lights up from deep within. I'm transported to my mum's car on a rainy day during the summer holidays in 1990.

I grew up in Liverpool, a short drive from a coastal town called Crosby. As beautiful as the beach is there, as a kid I associated it with rain, wind and being told it was too cold to get a screwball from the ice-cream van. So as the grey skies bombarded yet another day of the school holidays, my nine-year-old self wasn't particularly overjoyed at my mum's idea of an afternoon out as we pulled up in the car park.

'I thought we could get some fresh air,' she announced. Had she gone mad? I didn't want to seem rude, but my face spelt it out pretty clearly: 'Really?!'

Ahead of us through the windscreen, the River Mersey was a brownish grey. Some days, it can be glittering, moving like a gentle dance, but not that day. Behind us were the local swimming baths, which would have been an amazing alternative if only we'd come prepared. But there wasn't a hint of that in sight. Yet as I began to protest, my mum pulled out a pink striped beach bag she'd hidden under the passenger seat. 'Shall we?'

Had Christmas come early? Was it possible to make a wish and for it to come true so quickly? My mum had indeed come prepared: swimming costumes, towels, shampoo, the lot. We were really doing it. We were going swimming!

My memory hasn't held onto the actual swimming session clearly, but I know it would have involved lots of jumping in, practising handstands and generally being ecstatically happy to be having fun in the water with my mum. I do remember being allowed to buy crisps from the vending machine on the way out, with my mum saying, 'Swimming makes you hungry'. And more than thirty years later, whenever I'm hit by the smell of chlorine, I always think of this – all of it. I hear the rain battering down on the car. I see the pink striped beach bag. I feel my heart swell. It was such a great surprise and it's lodged deep inside, reminding me that I'm safe and loved.

'WHATEVER
STATE YOUR
SKY HAPPENS
TO BE IN,
IT'S ALWAYS
THERE.'

LET'S GO GLIMMER HUNTING

The power to find glimmers is within you. Going hunting for glimmers can be something you do independently or with a friend. Some people might find that their glimmers are deeply personal, with a few lighter-hearted ones scattered here and there. Others prefer to spread their joy, even if it's not met with anyone else who agrees. However you choose to hunt for glimmers, allow your creativity to be unleashed. They really are ... *everywhere*.

1.
Set yourself a goal of finding four glimmers every day.
Write them down before you go to sleep. Or message them to your co-hunter, awaiting their glimmers in return.

2.
Become more aware of scents.
Think about where you are likely to find your most favoured smells, from garlic cooking to the floral notes of a rose.

3.
Be mindful of all the sounds around you.
If you pause, even somewhere very quiet, you might be surprised at how sensitive your ears can be. Can you hear children laughing in the playground at the local school? The seagulls near the sea? The leaves rustling in the wind?

4.
Create a playlist and fill it with all the songs that make your heart sing.
There are NO rules with this one. From Bowie to Britney to Beethoven ... glimmer-shimmy to the dance floor. Or just to work!

5.
Pick up on people cues.
Notice when you've engaged in good, connected conversation. A great chat has the power to lift us out of a dark place. Maybe you really needed that pep talk, so be grateful to whoever allowed you to offload and feel lighter. Acknowledge that joke you heard beside the water cooler. Appreciate that person who elevates your mood. Strive to make these moments happen more often. And as a counterbalance, be aware of those who tend to trigger you. Be firm and shut it down. Don't invite their bad energy into your vibe.

GLIMMER BLOCK

In the same way that writers suffer from writer's block, it can be hard to find a glimmer if you're looking too hard. Putting yourself under immense pressure to feel fuzzy because you've seen a daffodil isn't magically going to have you twirling around the hills like Maria von Trapp. So, if you're staring at a blank page, struggling for a glimmer to fill its space, try some word association.

Here's an example. If I start with the word *awe* and allow that to prompt other thoughts, I get: grand, larger than life, mountain, fresh air, road trip, spectacular views, greenery, snowcaps, skiing...

It's worth remembering that nobody is judging you for these answers. Unless, maybe, you are. So stop. Quit the cringe and be kind to yourself! Lecture over.

Try it yourself with the following prompts:

Happy

....

....

Sweet

....

....

Connection

....

....

Funny

....

....

Tranquil

....

....

Light

....

....

Glee

....

....

Tasty

....

....

Love

....

....

Warmth

....

....

Now complete these sentences:

I get excited at the thought of

....

....

I feel energetic when I

....

....

I really care about

....

....

I get emotional when

....

....

I feel nostalgic about

....

....

If I could click my fingers and be anywhere right now, I'd

....

....

I love the smell of

....

....

I find it hilarious when

....

....

I am triggered by

....

....

The opposite to these triggers are

....

....

'The sun, — the bright sun, that brings back, not
light alone, but new life, and hope,
and freshness to man.'

CHARLES DICKENS
Oliver Twist

BIRTHDAY ✧
✧ GLIMMER

I've always felt a bit awkward on my birthday. Until this year.

For weeks leading up to my special day, I'd always get that sickly, anxious feeling. What should I do to make it special? What might others do to make it special? Who should I invite? Who do I not want to invite? What would make me happy? But then what would make everybody else happy?

Some people might be okay with being slowly – eerily – serenaded 'Happy Birthday'. Others might genuinely get a buzz from the type of crowd who breaks into harmonies with the final dragged-out notes. But we've got to admit, it's always a bit weird, right? I always want the ground to swallow me up whole, but I don't know why I'm so triggered by this. I do love the cake and candles bit – making a wish. It's a genuine moment to believe in magic, to hope, to think of the best thing you possibly can, followed by that gentle release into the universe as you blow. But back to the song ... eugh. Asking people *not* to sing, however, would make me feel a bit guilty – as if I wasn't grateful for their presence and their eagerness to celebrate, well, me.

A birthday can be – and, as we get older, is very likely to be – a pretty normal day. But there's this pressure to be in the best mood ever. You get asked if you're having a fabulous day, if you're being spoilt rotten, if you have your feet up, if you're celebrating with something sparkly ... and you have to say YES, no matter what the reality is. It can be tiring. Don't get me wrong, I've had some amazing parties. From *Mad Men*-themed dress-up soirées to karaoke in Soho at 3 am. Each time, though, I kind of wished I was at the exact same party, but not as the Birthday Gal. I wanted to be there to experience it, not lead it.

Anyway, a short while before my last birthday, I went to the cinema. I realized I hadn't been in ages. As I sat in the reclining seat and tucked into my popcorn (strictly salted), I felt that familiar gentle tingle of excitement as the trailers ended, the lights dimmed and the screen extended for the feature presentation. I loved it. How had I been away for so long? There's not a single movie I've not enjoyed at the cinema! I went to see *Jurassic Park* no less than five times. I even enjoyed *The Cable Guy*.

So I took the day off for my birthday and went to the cinema. At 10 am! I just decided to watch whatever was showing and, once again, I felt that lovely buzz in the seconds before the movie started. It didn't matter what I did afterwards – whether I threw a party or ordered a takeaway – because I'd found a glimmer in a day that had always given me unnecessary and inexplicable anxiety. And I got an extra kick from being in a cinema during the daytime!

Find your unexpected glimmer and make it an annual treat.

'MAKING A WISH AS YOU BLOW OUT BIRTHDAY CANDLES IS A GENUINE MOMENT TO BELIEVE IN MAGIC.'

BANTER
AND BOOKS

Fancy an insight into my WhatsApp habits? Here's the genuine transcript of a chit-chat I had with my pal, Lydia, recently. This is exactly how the conversation flowed, and it just goes to show that you can spot a glimmer absolutely anywhere, anytime, anyhow...

The next time you engage in some informal chit-chat, see if you can recognize what makes you smile or gives you fresh perspective. So often we gloss over these tiny moments and jump back into our worries and tight schedules. Treasure can be found; you just need to be prepared to hunt a little further to discover it.

Me:
You okay?

Lydia:
Had to go for a walk to clear my head.
Went to the shop and bought some
Maltesers and a glossy mag.

Me:
A glossy mag? Ha. What is this, 1998? LOL.

Lydia:
I swear, what a treat.

Me:
I bet.

Lydia:
Lying on the bed flicking through the pages.
Honestly, SUCH a treat.

Me:
Okay, you've made me wanna go
to the shop now.

Lydia:
Go. Get off your phone!

When was the last time you picked out a little magazine
for yourself? Turned the smooth pages while lying on
your tummy?

In the words of Margaret Atwood, 'I read for pleasure and
that is the moment I learn the most'.

'YOUR
PROBLEMS
START
TO FEEL
SMALLER IN
COMPARISON
TO THAT VAST
EXPANSE
OF SKY.'

THE SKY ✦

A mystery of limitless wonder... And yet, it's constant. Always there. A collective shelter for the universe.

If you're struggling to connect to your personal glimmers, keep it simple. Just look up. Focus on something that's everywhere, all around us – the sky.

Sometimes, looking up at the sky can just make us feel ... *better*. And do you know why? It's so wondrously big that it has the power to shrink stress. Sky-gazing can significantly benefit our wellbeing through its calming and meditative effect on the mind. It can also help to ground you by providing a strong sense of perspective; your problems start to feel smaller in comparison to that vast expanse of sky. (You might experience a similar sensation by looking at an imposing mountain range.)

> **Can you see thick, heavy white clouds?**
> **Or a bold and beautiful blue expanse?**

> **Are the stars splattered low and saying hello in a night sky?**
> **Or hidden behind the city's haze?**

Whatever state your sky happens to be, it's always there. Watch its colours, its moving clouds, its openness. You might spot a shooting star, or you might not, but you will reach a sense of calm ... and creativity! What can be found within those twinkling celestial pathways, you wonder? Your mind can run wild with curiosity. In fact, you might even sleep better. Artificial light pollution and digital screens don't do us any favours at bedtime. Exposing yourself to a bit of stargazing can help regulate your circadian rhythm. The light is natural; you're closer to nature.

If you've ever been camping, can you recall falling into a delightful slumber? This is because being outdoors increases the production of melatonin, a hormone that responds to darkness. Even if you live in the bright lights of the city, standing on your balcony or porch, or taking a minute to appreciate the view from a large window, could be just the tonic before snuggling under the covers.

Acknowledging a glimmer in the sky can really encourage us to slow down. In a fast-paced world, saddled with endless to-do lists, it's easy to lose sight of the bigger picture beyond our hectic little lives. Simply looking at a night sky filled with stars is awe-inspiring. In the most positive sense, we realize just how small we are. It fills us with generosity and perspective, and we feel compelled to release any sense of entitlement.

No matter where you stand on planet Earth, we all share the same sky. We are united.

'The wood was silent, still and secret in the evening drizzle of rain, full of the mystery of eggs and half-open buds, half unsheathed flowers. In the dimness of it all trees glistened naked and dark as if they had unclothed themselves, and the green things on earth seemed to hum with greenness.'

D. H. LAWRENCE
Lady Chatterley's Lover

AN AFTER- SCHOOL GLIMMER

When the ordinary meets the extraordinary.

When I pick my son up from school, I never ask, 'How was your day?' The question is too vague, too open-ended. Instead, I ask if his day was good, medium or bad. It provokes a more honest answer and creates a safe space for him to tell me if something is wrong.

Yesterday, my son told me he'd had a medium day. And that's fine. Not every day can be spectacular, and I was glad he didn't feel any pressure to tell me something amazing – or to admit to anything upsetting. We held hands and walked through the housing development behind his school. It's been a pretty long, wet winter and signs of spring haven't been too present this year. Yesterday, however, was a touch warmer and unexpectedly sunny after all the drizzle.

As we turned the corner, we passed an opening between two rows of houses. I caught a lovely glimpse of blue sky, which took me by surprise. I stopped and squeezed my son's hand, then told him to look up too.

We both smiled and talked about the two clouds we could see, plonked on top of that pretty blue sky. One was small and fluffy, and the other had a totally different texture, as if they belonged to two very different families. It was fun to spot, and for some reason it made us both chuckle. That small moment was all it took to transform our regular walk home from school into something more wonderful.

GABY'S GLIMMER

Find stillness by focusing on the small things.

TV presenter Gaby Roslin was close friends with the comedian Paul O'Grady, also known by the name of his alter ego, Lily Savage. A year after Paul passed away, Gaby still missed him and wished she could just call him.

Chatting to Anna Richardson on the *It Can't Just Be Me* podcast, Gaby explained how a friend had advised her to find relief from her sadness by paying close attention to something as simple as a leaf. Stopping and taking the time to study an apparently ordinary leaf would distract her for a moment – long enough to hold her interest, making her aware that every leaf is unique; no two are quite the same.

'And just for that split second, you've taken yourself out of the sadness, out of the loneliness, out of the worry, whatever it is ... And you just have that moment ... To yourself.'

'Then sometimes the immense
quiet of the dark blue at night with
the millions of stars waiting and
watching makes one sure; and
sometimes a sound of far-off music
makes it true; and sometimes a
look in some one's eyes.'

FRANCES HODGSON BURNETT
The Secret Garden

GLIMMERS ...
IN A NUTSHELL

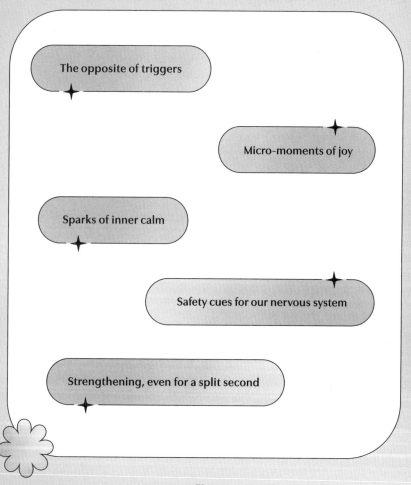

The opposite of triggers

Micro-moments of joy

Sparks of inner calm

Safety cues for our nervous system

Strengthening, even for a split second

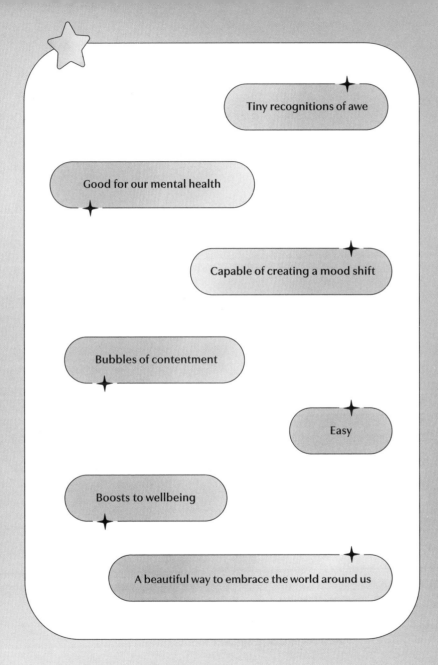

Tiny recognitions of awe

Good for our mental health

Capable of creating a mood shift

Bubbles of contentment

Easy

Boosts to wellbeing

A beautiful way to embrace the world around us

A BASKETFUL
OF GLIMMERS

Let's gather some simple pleasures that result in deep satisfaction.

While writing this book, I made a point of asking lots of people what their glimmers were. Whether it was a parent on the school run or a delivery driver at my front door, they all shared a moment of joy that was unique to them. Here's a selection to enjoy...

'My little girl's ponytail swaying from side to side as she skips around the park.'

'Scrunching litter into a ball and throwing it into the wastepaper basket successfully. Boom!'

'Eye contact with my best friend – when we don't have to say anything to each other to know exactly what the other is thinking.'

'Kitchen karaoke while I do the dishes. When nobody's listening, of course.'

'When I go for a run and pass by places that I enjoy hanging out with my family. Like running through the park, and thinking about the first time my son sat on those swings as a baby.'

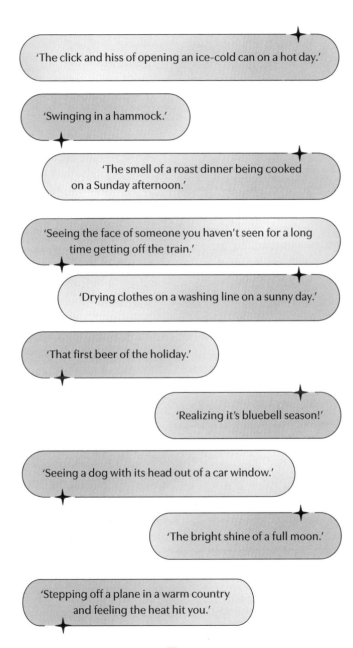

'The click and hiss of opening an ice-cold can on a hot day.'

'Swinging in a hammock.'

'The smell of a roast dinner being cooked on a Sunday afternoon.'

'Seeing the face of someone you haven't seen for a long time getting off the train.'

'Drying clothes on a washing line on a sunny day.'

'That first beer of the holiday.'

'Realizing it's bluebell season!'

'Seeing a dog with its head out of a car window.'

'The bright shine of a full moon.'

'Stepping off a plane in a warm country and feeling the heat hit you.'

I LIKE BIG PANTS AND I CANNOT LIE...

Or, the story of how I went from thong to strong.

Once upon a time, I was a thong girl. I could roll up a pair into a ball and manage a disappearing magic trick with ease, the garment was that minimal. I only owned three colours, too: nude, white and black. The black ones lasted the longest because once the elastic started to give, the white and nude looked like a battered old bit of string.

But, oh, those thongs! It was like being naked but knowing you definitely weren't naked all at once. I felt free and flexible and never worried about a dreaded VPL in any of my outfits. If my laundry was piling up and I was out of thongs, my other underpants were such a drag – so restricting, like having to wear a whole extra item of clothing. Ugh, what a faff.

Then, boom. I transitioned ... uncomfortably.

'SO HOORAY FOR BIG UNDERPANTS, I SAY. A PHYSICALLY COMFORTING EVERYDAY GLIMMER.'

When I fell pregnant, I believed my love of teeny-weeny thongs would be a blessing. They'd just carry on doing their *thong* (sorry, not sorry), taking care of delicately keeping below 'covered'. Even though I knew I was going to expand in size, the stretchy material would deal with that. It wasn't as if my thongs went anywhere near my belly, was it? Well, how wrong I was. Once my body started to change, so did the feeling of the thong. It felt … wrong. The back bit sagged down and the front part creased over. I was far too aware of the actual thong, which, let's face it, ain't the point of going down the thong route in the first place.

So I got some midi-type stretchy underwear, a few sizes bigger than usual, and accepted that this was another temporary change I'd have to go through while pregnant. But they either sagged, dug in, or managed to do both simultaneously. In a state of underwear despair (and we all know that when our underwear feels odd, our *everything* feels odd), I browsed BIG underpants. Realistically, none of the others were going to give me any comfort, so reluctantly, I went for it. I got the big pregnancy underpants that completely cover your tummy, the material stretching all the way to below my bra. Basically, an underpants bodysuit … eek.

Although, actually, not eek. It was, aahhhh! Any itch, dig, roll, sag … gone. All that remained was sheer glimmer-y comfort. I barely knew I was wearing any underpants (a nice lil' nostalgic glimmer from my thong days), and even more glimmers started to glow. I felt neat. Tucked in. Safe. Warm. My clothes fell elegantly over the giant underpants and I didn't have to pick, pull, tug or swivel them around every time I stood up. I vowed never to go back!

A few months after my baby was born I had to ditch my beloved maternity underwear, for obvious reasons. In purchasing replacements, I made a few mistakes along the way. I was so used to the miniature scale of thongs that I assumed a bikini cut or midi-shorts would be massive by comparison, and opted to give them a whirl. The tummy digs made a most unwelcome return. The rolling below my soft belly pouch occurred every time I sat or bent down. They made me SO aware of the flesh around my middle that I was most self-conscious about. So I picked up a pack of high-waisted full briefs. Hmm. Not so brief. This was a major garment, a whole chunk of fabric – Bridget Jones-esque in all its glory. I got cold feet. I couldn't possibly...

But I bought the damn things. Might as well try 'em.

As soon as the fabric covered my belly button and tucked gently around my waist, I heard the choirs sing 'Hallelujah!' I sat, I stood, I got down into a sumo squat and did a bit of downward dog. The underpants stayed put. It was lovely to slip my clothes on over my underwear and not have an under-annoyance chipping away at me all day long. And forget the old nude, white and black that used to dominate my underwear drawer – the big underpants were welcome in a delightful rainbow of polka dots, stripes, lacy trims and hot pink. Granny underpants these were NOT. Sure, I got nude for light summer dresses, and who doesn't love their black staples, but my thongs just didn't have enough thong to be anything but thong!

My transition into big underpants – surprisingly – made me feel more desirable, too. Hearing 'neat', 'tucked in' and 'safe' might have you sprinting to buy a diamanté-encrusted G-string, but I genuinely feel so much more attractive in my everyday clothes now. I recall how stressful it was growing up in the nineties, when low-waisted jeans and combat trousers were all the go – gossip magazines were forever shaming female celebrities by zeroing in on their 'muffin tops', and yet we were all lured into buying clothes that made this difficult to avoid.

So hooray for big underpants, I say. A physically comforting everyday glimmer. Whether you're singing the thong song or having a dance in big underpants, do what makes you happy.

Be comfortable. Be confident. Be you.

LET'S TAKE ✦ THE PRESSURE ✦ OFF

Do you ever feel like a victim of hidden advertising?

It seems that everywhere we look, we're secretly being sold how to do something or be somebody – partnered with so many contradictions. Stay in! Stop drinking! Go out! Have fun! An addiction to the scroll is fed with easy tips for weight loss, easy hacks to travel the world, and five easy steps to earning six figures a month. But why isn't any of this ... easy?

Hard truth: the only person putting this pressure on you, is you. Sure, others might try to steer you off-course, but *you* are *your* life. It's YOU vs YOU. Comparing yourself to anybody and everybody is your choice, so you also have the power to stop. Whatever makes you tick, whatever makes you smile, it's all yours. So give yourself a break...

'I'm too busy,' you cry, 'I have too much to do.' You're on a deadline so you can't make yourself a cup of lemon-and-ginger tea? You're in a meeting so you're unable to take a deep breath and inhale the gorgeous perfume you sprayed on your wrists this morning? Nobody will ever care about your career as much as you do. It's time to let go of pleasing others and start pleasing yourself.

You will shine.

'IT'S TIME TO LET GO OF PLEASING OTHERS AND START PLEASING YOURSELF.'

In fact, you already *do* shine. Your own light is effortless, even if it's hiding in the shadows right now. Remember, a glimmer is small, but it always glows. Don't try to be the sun. We all know how dangerous that big ball of fire can be. It's tempting to want bigger. To aspire to more. To have it all. A crazy-quick twenty minutes on Instagram will confirm this. But once we land back in our reality and look around, we can use our time on earth to create meaningful moments that come right out of the ordinary. Singing a funny song with your kid while they're in the bath. Making grilled cheese sandwiches for lunch. Chances are, you'll have already done something today that's more meaningful than you realize. You might feel a bit weird giving yourself a pat on the back, so take a deep, nourishing breath instead.

Hold onto your light. Even a twinkle matters.

GIVE
A LIL'
GLIMMER

As the kids in *Bugsy Malone* sang,
'You give a little love and it all comes back to you...'

Well, give a little glimmer and you'll get a glimmer
in return. It feels good to do good.

Don't worry if you can't donate money to charity or find
the time to volunteer. Good micro-deeds have a wonderful
habit of creating a snowball effect.

1.
A simple compliment goes a long way.
People remember those who make them feel special.

2.
Gift-wrapping can be therapeutic.
The scented candle might be for your friend, but you get to smooth down the paper, fold it neatly and enjoy the satisfaction of taping it together. Go crazy, add a bow!

3.
Cook for someone special.
What's your signature dish? Does it bring you joy to rustle up a lasagne or bake a sponge cake? Well, it's going to bring a whole lotta joy to those who get to eat it.

4.
Not everybody spots a rainbow in the sky.
So when you see one, share it.

5.
Listen.
Just listen. You might happen to be the glimmer in somebody else's day by simply listening to what they have to say.

6.
The same goes for a hug.
Hold that hug, linger a little longer there.

7.
And ask someone what their glimmers are.
Talking about them brings them to life!

LINGERING ✦
✦ GLIMMERS

If you had thirty minutes all to yourself, what would you do?

'What can be achieved in a mere half hour?' you ask. 'It's nothing. It might as well be ten minutes.' Well, it's not about the time frame itself; it's more about how you choose to use it.

We can all lose thirty minutes scrolling on our phones. It flashes by like lightning. And when we do this, we haven't been engaged in a singular activity, either; we've been flipping from app to app, watching self-help gurus and billionaires on podcasts, replying to messages, getting lost in last year's photos, obsessing over how much we've aged, how much weight we've gained. All until a greater distraction (usually in human form) drags us away from our idle, endless browsing – the doorbell rings, a colleague approaches you, the train arrives at your stop, a child demands a snack. Whoosh, that's your thirty minutes done and dusted. And the feeling we're often left with after those thirty minutes is far from satisfying.

As a teenager, I had a Saturday job at Woolworths (RIP ... browsing that store was full of glimmers). My shift allowed me to take a half-hour break. I would nip to the cafe across the street and get a baked potato. By the time I'd grabbed my purse, used the bathroom, queued for a spud and returned to the break room, I had a few minutes to gobble it down. I was always a bit late returning to the shop floor, piping-hot potato still undigested in my chest, and a telling-off by my manager awaiting me. So I started to take a packed lunch.

If there happened to be others in the break room, it was fun to chat (and cringe) about the latest work night out, but most of the time I was alone in there. Suddenly thirty minutes felt like a long time to sit in silence and eat my lunch, and if I took a book to work, it was absolute bliss. I'd savour every page and that short break became a highlight. A glimmer. I even started to leave a paperback at work, making that particular book exclusive to my precious break time. Like looking forward to a weekly episode of your favourite TV show.

Making improvements to your life – or yourself – doesn't have to be about making one big gesture. Doing small things every day – or even weekly – can add up to larger growth in the long run. Getting into the habit of utilizing thirty minutes to nuzzle into your glimmers may help to increase your confidence and reduce your stress levels, stabilizing your work–life balance. Ultimately, you'll see benefits far beyond the mere thirty minutes a week you spend channelling them.

So what can you do in a solid half hour? How would you love to glimmer-ize that time? Going to a yoga class or hitting the gym isn't what we're talking about here. You can't do either of those in thirty minutes (once you factor in the journey and taking a shower). And if you arrange to meet a friend for coffee, you're going to rush the catch-up and feel pretty disappointed when the end arrives abruptly. It's not about cramming in lots of activity. That's not the point. Instead, imagine you've been given a small trinket of time – just enough to find something that makes you feel satisfied.

Time is always a gift that most of us take for granted.

How about these for starters?

1.
Read a magazine.
A physical copy. Sit down, scour the pages, circle the things you love with a pen. You'll absorb the content without exposing yourself to more screen-time and you'll retain the information better because you won't be under pressure to check other apps and messages.

2.
Sort a drawer.
Just ONE. Remove the overwhelming thoughts telling you to sort out your entire life! Start with your underwear drawer. Use small dividers and roll your garments Marie Kondo-style. When the drawer is finished, breathe with a sense of achievement. You can do the next drawer tomorrow.

3.
Treat yourself.
Instead of trying to find a whole outfit and stressing out in the changing room, why not make a decision to buy yourself a lipstick or a new nail colour. Indulge in choosing the shade. Or is there a bakery you've been wanting to try? Pick a cake and enjoy.

4.
Free-write.
You don't have to be an aspiring novelist to write, freely, without any directions or constraints. Forget about grammar and spelling – just set a timer and start. Maybe have a prompt or question to get you started, then see where the writing takes you. Discover how you're feeling and what's on your mind!

5.
Watch a TED Talk.
They're like mini-lectures and usually around 20 minutes (so enough time to make a cup of tea, too!) You might learn something about yourself or be inspired into action, or simply gain new knowledge. But you have to be strict – resist the temptation to dip in and out of other apps, or turn all notifications off.

6.
Phone a friend.
If ever my best friend phones me, I always answer and say, 'Is everything okay?' Oh, how we've grown accustomed to text! But don't be afraid of speaking. Hearing a voice you adore on the other end of the line can give you the best boost. What's more, you have them all to yourself, for a good ol' chat, for half an hour.

7.
Watch the world go by.
Slip away from your desk and find yourself a comfy spot or a pretty view. Soak up the scene. People watch. Pop in your earphones and listen to your fave playlist.

8.
Puzzle mania.
Get yourself a book filled with Sudoku, crosswords, word-searches and logic puzzles. Paper is conducive to attention and engagement. Studies have shown that our brains actually process and store information better offline. Don't forget a pen ... and no Googling the answers!

9.
Revisit the nineties and noughties.
Watch one full episode without distraction of something like *Friends*, *The Office* or *Sex and the City*. You're spoilt for choice. But decide on what show in advance. Don't waste your thirty minutes surfing the streaming services.

10.
Play the piano.
Or the violin. Or simply sing! Beginners are advised to practise regularly for fifteen to thirty minutes to improve. You're never too old to learn how to play a musical instrument.

'MAKING
IMPROVEMENTS
TO YOUR LIFE —
OR YOURSELF —
DOESN'T HAVE
TO BE ABOUT
MAKING ONE
BIG GESTURE.'

SHINY,
HAPPY
GLIMMERS

The smell of nostalgia can be sweet.

What glimmers can glow from behind those John Lennon-style rose-tinted spectacles?

If you're a millennial like me, your childhood summers were pumped with girl power and 'Return of the Mack'. You borrowed CDs and recorded songs onto cassette, memorizing all the lyrics printed inside the album sleeve. And if it rained, you were forced to stay inside glued to the same TV shows as your friends (cue the theme to *The Fresh Prince of Bel Air*).

Trends from previous decades come and go, especially in fashion and music. Inspiration is taken from icons of the past, revitalized to suit the modern era with a nod to their original genius. Look around. Young people are rocking a nineties clothing revival and *Friends* merch is so down with the kids that it's become retro-classic. But what about lifestyle? Can thinking back to yesteryear give us a glimmer or two?

In the mid-nineties I remember getting a mini portable TV for Christmas. It was the size of a Game Boy and operated on four AA batteries with a long adjustable aerial. Getting a decent picture took forever, and by the time I'd tuned into *Neighbours* at five thirty-five, the six o'clock news had started and the batteries had worn out. I dreamed of a sci-fi world where I could watch anything, anywhere, anytime. But that seemed absurd.

Be careful what you wish for, 'Kidz of the 9Ts'. Technology has since created a generation of impatience. We expect instant results and immediate gratification. We face a constant struggle with the never-ending choices on offer. We can get anything – *anything* – with one touch. And if we can't, oh boy, we don't half complain about it. How are we expected to tune into our glimmers if we're refreshing our smartphones, wondering why the duck gyoza delivery hasn't arrived within the fifteen-minute window as promised?

I remember going to see *Who Framed Roger Rabbit?* I loved it so much and was desperate to see it again. So when a making-of documentary came on TV, I recorded it, watching it on repeat just to catch snippets of the actual movie. This wasn't so bad in the end. I discovered a love for behind-the-scenes footage that sang to my inner movie geek. I still can't resist a featurette, a blooper or the chance to see an alternative ending.

So instead of getting frustrated when things don't instantly meet our demands, could we just allow them to happen naturally? A bit like how things used to be. Can we rely on technology less? Increase our tolerance for waiting? We might just find a glimmer hiding there, masked by today's need for speed.

'ALLOW
THINGS TO
HAPPEN
NATURALLY
AND YOU MIGHT
JUST FIND
A GLIMMER
HIDING THERE'

1.
It's okay to be bored.

And it's so underrated. Look out the window when you're on a bus. If it's raining, watch the drips wriggle down the pane like snakes that join up with each other (I bet you always did this as a child). Being bored as a kid in the old days was actually filled with mindfulness, not just playfulness. I used to cut shapes out of empty breakfast-cereal boxes and made stuff using adhesive tape. I tried out new hairstyles and raided my mum's old earrings box. I made up dance moves. Did handstands. Doodled with paper and felt tip pens. Daydreamed.

2.
Nip to the shop.

Online shopping has become an ingrained habit. But nipping out to actual shops gets your body moving. You can double it up with lunch or coffee with a friend. You don't have time? Well, sure, online shopping is quicker ... or is it? How long have you actually been surfing the web for that product? Have you even found it yet? Or have you been distracted by another product? When you get out to get stuff, you might be pleasantly surprised at what you find.

3.
Postcards.

We rarely receive a postcard, but they're still sold everywhere!
Buy a few stamps. Let your kids choose some postcards,
perhaps while browsing a bookshop. Let them decide who
they'd love to send them to, then write them together and
post them. Who would you love to surprise with a simple
hello or a daft joke? This small, rather old-fashioned idea has
a fabulous end goal – guaranteed to make the person on the
receiving end smile. Glimmers all round.

4.
Use the phone.

Don't text or message. Always phone whoever you need to
speak to. It's a win–win because it's still the most efficient
way to communicate. You hear tone of voice. You get an
instant response. No crossed wires in sight. Let your kids
hear you speaking to somebody instead of tapping on your
smartphone. Enjoy the simplicity of chatting; no embarrassing
camera angles, no bad wi-fi, no awkward typos!

5.
Be lazy.

Because it's likely you do A LOT. So don't feel bad about doing
nothing. Make baked beans on toast for dinner. Listen to Pulp,
Motown, or The Beatles. Watch a classic movie – maybe a
musical with Gene Kelly. Only bother moving when you want
to snuggle into a more comfortable position.

'With freedom, flowers, books,
and the moon, who could not
be perfectly happy?'

OSCAR WILDE
De Profundis

MY *MY GIRL* GLIMMER ✦

How to find sunshine on your cloudy days.

When that famous bass line by the Temptations kicks off the Motown classic 'My Girl', I catch a glimmer. It doesn't matter what mood I'm in before the song comes on, I always have a micro-moment of joy when I hear the opening lyrics: 'I got sunshine on a cloudy day...'

Here's why.

In February 1992, there was only one thing eleven-year-old girls in my town were talking about – a new movie starring Macaulay Culkin, set in, oddly, a funeral parlour. During play time at school, conversations revolved around this, and only this – in between ballet exercises at the barre, at hang-outs with Happy Meals, on bike rides to the shop and back. The UK had been hit with *My Girl* mania, especially for those of us who happened to be the exact same age as Macaulay or the newcomer Anna Chlumsky, playing the iconic roles of Thomas J. Sennett and Vada Sultenfuss.

Much of the chit-chat involved showing-off though. This came from those who had seen it – or, more precisely, been allowed to go and see it. *My Girl* hype had meant that a lot of the themes presented in the movie had been leaked, and since the protagonist was an eleven-year-old girl, some of the content seemed a little mature. There had never been a movie like it. And while much of what happened to young Vada was completely normal, a Hollywood scene about starting your period was not. On top of that, there was a lot of talk about death and, heartbreakingly, the death of a child. My mum's opinion on this was clear. Despite asking and asking to be allowed to see it, 'Because it's not fair, everybody else has seen it', I was met with a Hard No.

That was how it was back then. If you wanted to see a movie, you simply had to see it at the cinema. It would be months – a year even – until it became available to rent from the video shop. Less content was being produced, too. So if something big was released, it was everywhere, taking all the advertising space. I couldn't escape *My Girl*, or this constant feeling of being left out of the coolest club in town. All I could do was listen as my peers sang 'Do Wah Diddy Diddy', and watch them fake-cry as they quoted, 'Put his glasses on!'

Then one afternoon, my dad had to go and pick up some tickets from the Civic Hall. Semi-pro comedians played there on Friday nights and local dance schools performed their annual showcases during the week. He asked if I wanted to go with him for the drive and I was happy to, especially since the Civic Hall was next door to the library. Once outside the Civic Hall, my dad stopped and looked across the busy road, scrunching up his eyes and pretending his eyesight was failing him.

'What does that say?,' he asked me, pointing at the cinema in the distance.

I gave a pre-teen huff and shrugged.

'I can't work out what it says,' he went on. 'What's showing?'

Another huff. '*My Girl*,' I said through gritted teeth, as if being forced to say these words was the cruellest of punishments. The world was against me.

'Oh,' my dad said lightly, 'shall we go and see it?'

I looked at him in disbelief. 'I'm not allowed!'

'Come on,' he said, giving me a wink. 'Let's go now. It starts in ten minutes.'

My throat went dry. I burst into tears. I was about to join THE gang. Belong. In that moment, I felt so seen. So heard! I threw my arms around my dad crying, 'Really? REALLY?!'

My Girl is one of those movies I've since watched again and again. When I hear the song, I get hit with nostalgic happiness, remembering the joy of crossing the road and buying a ticket from the kiosk to see the movie – secretly – with my dad. And as the bass comes in with the three-note riff, I'm forever reminded of what my dad did for me, allowing me access into the *My Girl* club, understanding that the world revolved around very specific things for an eleven-year-old girl, even if it was against my mum's wishes...

My dad, on the other hand, probably doesn't have much of a glimmer at this memory. He hadn't done his research. Wasn't clued up on the plot. Instead, he just sat through the entire movie feeling awkward, entirely out of his comfort zone. This was topped off with having to console me when the sad scenes got crazy heavy. Oh, I cried and ugly cried – sobbed all the way home in the car. I wasn't the first kid to be devastated at what happens in *My Girl* and I certainly wouldn't be the last. We arrived home, my face red and blotchy, my nose streaming. And when my dad had to admit where we'd been, my mum simply said, 'You see? I told you not to go!'

'IT DOESN'T
MATTER WHAT
MOOD I'M IN
BEFORE THE
SONG COMES ON,
I ALWAYS HAVE A
MICRO-MOMENT
OF JOY WHEN
I HEAR THE
OPENING LYRICS.'

GLIMMER-FIX FIVES

The Olympic symbol is made up of five rings of equal size. Coco Chanel's favourite number was five, and in 1921 she released her perfume Chanel No. 5 on 5 May, the fifth month. There are five Spice Girls. Wolfgang Amadeus Mozart was only five years old when he wrote his first known composition, a Minuet and Trio in G major.

Expand on this theme and forecast feelings of happiness by writing down some of your personal top fives, with a few nods to nostalgia. This exercise can give you the push to press play on that fave film or to pop in your earphones and listen to that awesome album. Within your collection of favourites, you're sure to find a glimmer or two. You can then refer back to these lists whenever you need a go-to for glimmers in the future.

TOP FIVE CHILDHOOD MOVIES

1.

....

....

2.

....

....

3.

....

....

4.

....

....

5.

....

....

TOP FIVE RECENT MOVIES

1.

....

....

2.

....

....

3.

....

....

4.

....

....

5.

....

....

TOP FIVE ALBUMS

1.

....

....

2.

....

....

3.

....

....

4.

....

....

5.

....

....

'YOU CAN
THEN REFER
BACK TO
THESE LISTS
WHENEVER YOU
NEED A GO-TO
FOR GLIMMERS
IN THE FUTURE.'

TOP FIVE FOODS

1.

....

....

2.

....

....

3.

....

....

4.

....

....

5.

....

....

TOP FIVE SONGS

1.

....

....

2.

....

....

3.

....

....

4.

....

....

5.

....

....

TOP FIVE ITEMS OF CLOTHING

1.

....

....

2.

....

....

3.

....

....

4.

....

....

5.

....

....

TOP FIVE BOOKS

1.

....

....

2.

....

....

3.

....

....

4.

....

....

5.

....

....

TOP FIVE DESSERTS

1.

....

....

2.

....

....

3.

....

....

4.

....

....

5.

....

....

TOP FIVE PLACES TO HANG OUT

1.
....
....

2.
....
....

3.
....
....

4.
....
....

5.
....
....

TOP FIVE DESTINATIONS VISITED

1.

....

....

2.

....

....

3.

....

....

4.

....

....

5.

....

....

TOP FIVE PEOPLE WHO MAKE ME LAUGH

1.
....
....

2.
....
....

3.
....
....

4.
....
....

5.
....
....

'WITHIN
YOUR
COLLECTION
OF FAVOURITES,
YOU'RE SURE
TO FIND A
GLIMMER
OR TWO.'

TOP FIVE PEOPLE WHO 'GET' ME

1.

....

....

2.

....

....

3.

....

....

4.

....

....

5.

....

....

TOP FIVE TV SHOWS

1.
....

....

2.
....

....

3.
....

....

4.
....

....

5.
....

....

TOP FIVE CELEBRITY CRUSHES

1.

....

....

2.

....

....

3.

....

....

4.

....

....

5.

....

....

TOP FIVE GAMES

1.

....

....

2.

....

....

3.

....

....

4.

....

....

5.

....

....

TOP FIVE ACTIVITIES

1.

....

....

2.

....

....

3.

....

....

4.

....

....

5.

....

....

TOP FIVE COLOURS

1.

....

....

2.

....

....

3.

....

....

4.

....

....

5.

....

....

SHIFTING ✦
✦ THE FOCUS

Our habits become our life, so what kind of life do you want?

I wonder if the pandemic has helped us to recognize glimmers more often. Time slipped away far too quickly. We lost years, and the back and forth of 'can we, can't we' left a deep, anxious scar. I fear time will rob me again, when I least expect it. But I try to use this to my advantage by making the most of every moment. This isn't easy when I'm unloading the washing machine or rushing to make packed lunches for the kids in the morning, but there used to be such a focus on the future, what we were going to do next. I've now experienced what it feels like to be stuck inside the unknown, to live right in the present – something I'd regularly lost sight of.

During the pandemic, I stopped aiming so high, wishing instead to settle for oodles of normality. I just wanted my kids to get through a full term at school, to see my family without navigating any bizarre rules, and to be able to wander into a restaurant and get a table without having made a reservation weeks in advance. So even now, when these 'normal' things happen, my heart can soar. Or perhaps it's relief. As the UK broadcaster and TV presenter Evan Davis famously reflected, 'It's not a bad idea to occasionally spend a little time thinking about things you take for granted. Plain everyday things.'

Which is what many of us did during COVID. There was nothing to do, nowhere to go, and people we weren't allowed to see. So we looked at the plain everyday things and tried to find the magic in them. Regular meal times became theme nights: Taco Tuesdays, Pizza Fridays. Going for a walk became an event. Finding a bench with a nice view to eat a sandwich became the highlight of the day. It was one hell of a miserable time, and we were forced to lower our expectations, but we also discovered the ability to spot glimmers lighting up the darkness.

Siri Steinmo is a behavioural scientist who works in the UK and the US. She explains that if we deliberately focus our attention on positive things, then we experience tangible benefits. 'We must look towards anything that can make us happy. Look at all we're grateful for. Glimmers are akin to the concept of gratitude, which has a strong evidence-base for improving wellbeing.' Those who practise gratitude not only tend to be happier people, but this mindset can also be contagious. 'When you start to notice things that make you happy and point them out, others begin to notice them too.'

In our fast-paced modern world, our attention is constantly pulled in many different directions. Choice is no longer 'this' or 'that'. Just look at Netflix. Oh, no. Look at Prime. Actually, look at them both – *and* Disney+, *and* Apple TV+ *and* Now TV. By the time you decide what to watch it's time to brush your teeth and go to bed. You might also remember to buy that face cream online, just before you nod off. So you open the browser on your phone, see a selection of similar face creams on offer, and suddenly you can't figure out what to buy. You probably give up and scroll through other stuff for a bit – maybe answer a work email to save you doing it in the morning. You then decide to read, but can't quite decide which book to pick up of the three you've had on the go for months, stacked up beside your bed. There's always a plethora of avenues lying ahead of us, and we venture down too many of them – often all at once.

According to Siri, focusing on a glimmer can really help to cut through all this noise. 'Recognizing something that makes you happy will slow down your thinking and encourage you to be aware of the present moment.'

In his book *Four Thousand Weeks: Time Management for Mortals*, the British author and journalist Oliver Burkeman writes, 'When you get to the end of your life, the sum total of all the things you paid attention to will have been your life.' So what we choose to pay attention to really matters.

Siri makes the same point, reminding us of the harsh – and somewhat embarrassing – reality that many of us face: 'If you fill your life with paying attention to just doomscrolling, that is your life! We can focus too much time on calendar checking. We become obsessed with thinking about what's next on the to-do list. We fret about falling behind with this, with that, with the other, and we are never actually here now.' Siri admits that this is something she's guilty of herself. To help her stay on track she has a calendar notification on her phone that reminds her at 1 pm every day to slow down and look around.

Wouldn't it be better to spend our lives paying attention to nicer things? Allow those nice things to be our life? Siri's advice is to make an adjustment. To think a little differently and thereby shift the focus. This practice is the very opposite of endless, distracted scrolling, which numbs our brains and shuts us off. Glimmer-spotting is the antidote – it motivates us to be fully present, aware and engaged. 'If we start to think, "This is amazing, I'm just sitting here with my family and everyone is just giggling," then *THAT* becomes our life.'

'THERE'S ALWAYS A PLETHORA OF AVENUES LYING AHEAD OF US, AND WE VENTURE DOWN TOO MANY OF THEM — OFTEN ALL AT ONCE.'

PAUSE, ✦
INHALE,
✦ HOLD ON

'The days are long, but the years are short.' – Gretchen Rubin

These words were written by the American author and 'happiness expert' Gretchen Rubin, inspired by the realization one day that the bus ride to take her young daughter to school – something she'd viewed as a bit of a chore, but was filled with moments of wonder for her daughter – in fact constituted parenthood, her daughter's childhood. Life itself.

This phrase is often quoted by parents, including an elderly lady who was standing behind me in the supermarket check-out queue a few years ago. My toddler was restless and trying to climb out of the trolley; every minute felt like an hour. As the customers ahead of me bagged up their shopping or unloaded their groceries onto the conveyor belt, I tried offering her a biscuit, a banana, a packet of teddy-bear-shaped snacks, then (begrudgingly) a chocolate bar, followed inevitably by my phone. I felt like a total failure when I couldn't even bribe her to sit still with YouTube Kids. The lady behind me smiled kindly and, with a wisdom I don't yet own, patted my arm and said, 'The days are long, but the years are short.'

I've since come to appreciate the profound truth in this apparently simple saying.

December 2022 was my daughter's preschool Nativity play. It was as normal as normal can be. The entire thirty minutes was quintessentially festive, from tinsel-headed angels to a wonky donkey and Mary's headscarf falling off again and again. There was the child screaming the words with bold confidence. And another child who had to be handed over to mama for cuddles when it all became a bit too much. Meanwhile, the nursery teacher clip-clopped about the stage in high heels and dangly earrings, her well-seasoned routine of encouraging energy being a major part of the performance. When she prompted Mary to have a little cry because there was no room at the inn, Mary declared to the audience, 'I'm not crying because I'm not sad!' And as the pianist played the final chord of 'We Wish You a Merry Christmas' to raucous applause, the head teacher thanked everybody involved. On the way out, I acknowledged her and we shared a smile...

...Because exactly one year previously, the Christmas performance had been cancelled, as had been the case at schools all over the world. COVID was still so very present in our lives, and weeks of hard work were to be captured on camera instead and shared by parents online. I had contacted the head teacher to see if the children could perform outdoors, or do several performances for smaller, socially distanced audiences. I'd offered to help in any way. Omicron was about to burst onto the scene, but as a parent, all you want for your child is a sense of normality, and an end-of-year performance is a rite of passage. With a heavy heart, she'd had to say no. 'Next year,' she promised, but how far away that felt...

'ANNUAL EVENTS CAN OFTEN GIVE US A WAKE-UP CALL, SHOWING US HOW OUR LIVES CAN ZOOM PAST IN A FLASH.'

...Until that moment a year later when we smiled at one another. A glimmer. Those 365 days had passed us by in the blink of an eye. Sandwiched in between, there had been sleepless nights, anxious days, financial struggles, hot summer months, waiting for test results and muddling through toddler tantrums. Yet, despite all of this, the Earth had completed another trip around the sun. Suddenly we were all a year older, a year wiser. And there we were at the Nativity play. In person. Something I'd become convinced would never happen, had happened. Without a countdown. Without anticipation. It came ... and it went.

Annual events can often give us a wake-up call, showing us how our lives can zoom past in a flash. If there are certain colleagues you only see at a certain conference once a year, time spent together might start rolling into one. You say things like, 'Gosh, has it really been a year?' And you feel as if you only caught up with them yesterday. How is this possible when you've had so many long, testing days in between?

There are daily meetings that you dread and endure, feeling like they'll drag on for ever. Waiting for ages at a red traffic light can make your blood boil, make you wonder if it's in fact broken. Having a newborn constantly feeding when you're exhausted can make sleep seem like an impossible goal. Trying to get your little one's shoes on without a wrestling match makes you wonder how you'll ever leave the house again. Waiting for that phone call, that email, that delivery...

But it's while we're waiting that the year actually happens. A ballerina doing a pirouette.

As a kid, you're itching for your independence. It's like in the movie *Big*, when Josh Baskin makes a wish on a fortune-telling machine at a carnival. What does he wish for? To be BIG, of course. Able to access all the things that he believes are out of reach for a twelve-year-old. Likewise, I remember just wanting to get my high-school years over and done with so I could go to drama school. And as much as I had a blast at drama school, I couldn't wait to graduate, get an agent and move to London. I was always striving for the bigger picture, taking little notice of where I was in the present. I stuck around in toxic relationships, waiting to experience some sort of epiphany and for things to change for the better. Then when I became single, I longed to find love again; instead of taking the time to heal, I wished that time away. As Andy Bernard (played by Ed Helms) says in the finale of *The Office*, 'I wish there was a way to know you were in the good old days before you've actually left them.'

When my first baby was born, I was too exhausted to 'enjoy every minute' like all the handwritten messages inside the congratulations cards urged me to. I would look at mums pushing prams with slightly older babies, who perhaps didn't need feeding ten times a day anymore and slept for longer than forty-five minutes, and I'd think, 'I can't wait until he's that age.' Then when he reached that age and started weaning, I'd see older kids eating a sandwich and think, 'I can't wait until he's learnt how to eat rather than chuck it all over the floor.'

When my second baby arrived, I found each gruelling stage easier, in the knowledge that 'this too shall pass'. My previous experiences had granted me some wisdom. I accepted downtime, although it was rare. I tried to see a funnier side to the chaos, knowing I'd look back on this short, tiring spell and weirdly enough, pine for it. But I still couldn't enjoy every minute. I had not one but two little ones who needed me and if I could have torn myself into two for them, I would have. The waiting kicked in again. I'd stare at the clock, willing my husband to get home from work so he could help me.

Sometimes, he would be just ten minutes from home, but waiting to hear his key in the door felt like ten hours. I wished for my kids to be old enough to play with each other...

And now, they are. When my daughter sweetly sings Christmas songs to herself in the car no matter what month of the year we're in, and my son mindlessly joins in with her, I want to freeze time. I want to hold that smile in my heart tight, forever. When I see them practising cartwheels together, I wish for slow motion so that I can stare, rather than find my phone to film it.

So while we're constantly seeking the next step, climbing that steep mountain, unable to get a glimpse of the peak, the world keeps spinning. Even the good stuff we plan makes us scramble through, sprinting towards the dates in our diaries. You can't wait to see your best friend from college for drinks next Saturday. You booked tickets for that musical ages ago and are counting down the days until you finally get to see it. You're ordering Thai takeout tonight and you just need to get through a hectic afternoon before you can relax and devour it. We seem to live in a society that's desperate for certainty – about what's coming next, hoping things will get better.

But what if we embraced the uncertainty? Can we take a moment just to breathe and accept that things might not turn out as we want them to? Your best friend might cancel drinks next Saturday. Your kids might always fight. You might not get that promotion, but you might get a better offer elsewhere that wasn't even on your radar. You might never fix the problems in your relationship, and you might be much happier if you walk away. You might sit down and realize, I don't fancy Thai tonight, I'll order pizza instead. And it turns out to be delicious.

Enjoying the uncertainty might grant us more time – it's unlikely to pass us by because we're focused on the moment rather than the future goal. And perhaps, when your day feels long, tell yourself that this is an opportunity to pause. To catch a glimmer. Of course that's easier said than done when I have to drag my cranky kids to school in the rain, but one day they'll be too old to hold my hand. They'll get themselves from A to B without my help at all. And at that point I'll see a struggling parent in the supermarket, hitting a wall with every attempt at bribery, and I'll gently say to them, 'The days are long, but the years are short.'

'CAN WE TAKE
A MOMENT
JUST TO
BREATHE
AND ACCEPT
THAT THINGS
MIGHT NOT
TURN OUT AS
WE WANT
THEM TO?'

LET'S REFLECT ON...

You.

Self-reflection, or personal contemplation, means taking the time to meditate and evaluate your behaviours, thoughts, attitudes, motivations and desires. It's an important step in truly understanding yourself. The following suggestions provide some topics to get you started.

Who inspires you

- This person might be related to you, a newfound friend or even a celebrity.

- A motivational speaker, an expert, a doctor, a local artist.

- Or are you driven by the actions of a character from a book or movie? Perhaps they encouraged you to look at life differently, to see a fresh perspective. Fact can often be found within fiction.

What actions influence you

- Make a list of activities that tick your boxes. Things that help you feel satisfied. Nourished.

- Acknowledge these activities, whether it's playing a sport with friends or sorting out your kitchen cupboards.

- Make time for this often.

What motivates you

- Pay attention to specific tasks and how they make you feel. What gives you a sense of accomplishment? When do you feel like you're making progress?

- Motivation comes in all shapes and sizes. Going for a 5K run might put one person in the right mindset for a big meeting, whereas hearing the sound of the sea might spark another's creativity.

'MAKE A LIST
OF ACTIVITIES
THAT TICK YOUR
BOXES. THINGS
THAT HELP YOU
FEEL SATISFIED.
NOURISHED.'

How you grow

- Trying new things can be scary. Or you might not feel like you have the time to indulge. But discovering new passions, interests and potential skills allows you to grow.

- Stumbling upon new ideas is a glimmer in itself!

- Add to existing glimmers ... there's no limit.

What excites you

- Whenever you feel energized or truly alive, remember to take note!

- What are you doing to ignite these positive emotions?

Recognizing patterns

- Take note of how certain activities or experiences consistently bring you joy.

- Do these patterns tend to occur in particular settings or with certain people?

- Recognizing patterns means you can increase the chances of catching a glimmer.

GIVE ✦ YOURSELF A GLIMMER

Self-love should be big, but it can start with something small.

It's well documented that daily rituals such as morning meditation, journaling our thoughts and drinking lots of water are good for our mental health and wellbeing. But you're not alone if you find this overwhelming. I hear you.

Something as simple as deep breathing can feel like a chore, no matter how much harmony it might add to my day. I'm more than aware that I should sleep for eight hours a night, limit my sugar intake and rise early to make my days more productive. My body needs to stretch, to move, to strengthen, to rest, to stretch again...

Seriously, it's not that I'm unaware of all these important dos and don't's. But have you ever tried to keep up with all these rituals, pushing to find the joy it will all bring, yet been left feeling like a bit of a failure? The motivation to journal happy thoughts is at level zero. You skip those extra glasses of water because you're going on a long car journey. You forget to do those lunchtime squats because you got carried away at your desk and just wanted to push through. Cue mega-disappointment in self.

Glimmers, thank goodness, don't carry this weight. They're lighter on the mind, guilt-free. Experiencing a glimmer can often be so unexpected, such a surprise that it can shake off negative thoughts about not hitting 10K steps. But as you'll know by now, not all glimmers are spontaneous – you have the power to make them happen. Let your hugs linger. Make eye contact that isn't fleeting. When you pause in the moment, you can create magic. Just make the choice to do so. On the following pages I've made some suggestions that are almost guaranteed to bring rewards.

Rewatch favourite TV shows

Choosing a new show to watch might not seem like a difficult decision to make, especially after a long day at the office or once the kids are asleep having made it through the usual bedtime negotiations. But with such an overwhelming – infinite – number of choices at our disposal, indecisiveness can negate unwinding on the sofa. It drains our good energy.

New York-based clinical psychologist Dr Sabrina Romanoff believes that watching a comforting, familiar movie or TV show can eliminate these negative feelings and bring us to a place of safety. As she explains, 'It protects against disappointment and provides predictability and the illusion of control over your environment.'

Rewatching favourite films or TV shows can:

- Feel like revisiting old (fictional) friends.

- Allow you to form imaginary relationships and develop a sense of connection.

- Leave you free of the pressure to follow through on this connection because it's not real.

- Fill a social or romantic void in a comforting environment.

- Remind you of why you love a particular story, providing reassurance of who you are.

- Evoke similar experiences to how you feel when you think about people you love.

- Eliminate decision fatigue.

So there's nothing wrong with watching *Dirty Dancing* ... again.

'WHEN YOU
PAUSE IN THE
MOMENT, YOU
CAN CREATE
MAGIC.'

Pet a pet

A furry animal is a ninja of positive power. Pets are delightfully non-judgemental companions and it's just so lovely having another life beside you, breathing with you.

Stroking or cuddling your pet can:

- Reduce anxiety.

- Remind you to live in the present, as they do.

- Stop you worrying about tomorrow, and instead encourage you to enjoy the moment that they're clearly so invested in.

- Give you a sense of purpose – your pet needs you.

- Simply make you smile.

- Provide a pleasure that ignites the senses.

- Elevate levels of the 'happy hormones' serotonin and dopamine, which calm the mind and enable you to feel pleasure.

Play it again, Sam

It's a great feeling when your favourite song comes on the radio or is played at a party. You might have it featured on a playlist and, when that song kicks in, you get a glorious rush of emotions, your whole body tingling. There are no rules stating how many times you're allowed to listen to a certain song. So play it. Again. And again.

That favourite song can:

- Shift your emotions to a better place.

- Trigger dopamine, serotonin and what's known as the 'love hormone', oxytocin.

- Lower levels of the stress hormone cortisol.

- Calm, soothe and put your body into a state of relaxation.

- Remind you of who you are, helping to shape your identity.

- Take you on a trip down memory lane.

- Help you to express difficult emotions.

- Regulate your breathing.

- Make you want to dance, sway or close your eyes and be sucked into the moment.

The six-second kiss

A quick kiss can be nice, but a bit of a habit. Giving or receiving a peck on the cheek happens in the blink of an eye; it doesn't allow for any delicious rush. Extending that kiss to six seconds, however, can provide numerous benefits, according to psychologist and marriage researcher Dr John Gottman. Six seconds, he says, is long enough to experience a moment of connection with your partner, and it can also be a good exercise in mindfulness.

A six-second kiss
(or a twenty-second hug) can:

- Trigger oxytocin, creating a sense of safety and bonding.

- Reduce cortisol.

- Be self-soothing.

- Improve intimacy.

- Build fondness.

- Create a ritual of connection and prolong your relationship.

Six seconds is hardly any time at all, yet it has the potential to keep you glowing inside for much longer … with minimal effort required!

LOOK UP ✦

We have stopped looking up.

And yet we're forever looking ahead: at the calendar, at the deadline, at the long weekend. Just hop aboard a train. It's rare to see hard copies of books being read, never mind passengers looking out the window. Everybody is looking down. Walking to the shops, looking down. Sitting in the park, looking down. Socializing in bars, looking down. Now, so often, two friends will have a conversation with one another, in real life, while looking down and typing multiple conversations with others. When was the last time you looked up and into the distance, stretching a little further beyond?

From the window in my kitchen, I can see lots of trees. In truth, it's easy to take them all for granted. They've always been there. But if I lift my eyes up from my laptop, I notice how many different kinds there are, gathered like friends at a party. The shades of green vary, too, and when I look closer, further, I see so many different hues that it's an injustice to ever just describe them as 'green'.

I look up a little higher and spot a tall tree poking out. It sways gently, the branches breathing out and in, out and in, reminding me of a pair of lungs, alive. Each tree moves in its own fashion, although they're blown by the same wind. Like people dancing in a nightclub. I am really relishing this quiet, focused moment. The more I look, the more I see. I find myself taking a deep, nourishing breath. I feel amazing.

And all I did was look up.

'WHEN WAS
THE LAST TIME
YOU LOOKED
UP AND INTO
THE DISTANCE,
STRETCHING A
LITTLE FURTHER
BEYOND?'

OFF THE TOP OF YOUR HEAD part 2

Earlier in this book (page 40), you might have written down three glimmers that instantly came to mind. Now see if you can make a longer list. You might have noticed the sensation when biting into your favourite food. Taken note of that hilarious comment your friend made. Melted at something your child tried to say. Heard a theme tune that transported you back to your adolescence.

Are you tuning into your glimmers a little more?

1.

....
....
....
....
....
....

2.

....
....
....
....
....
....

3.

....

....

....

....

....

....

4.

....

....

....

....

....

....

5.

....

....

....

....

....

....

6.

....

....

....

....

....

....

7.

....

....

....

....

....

....

8.

....

....

....

....

....

....

9.

....

....

....

....

....

....

10.

....

....

....

....

....

....

11.

....

....

....

....

....

....

12.

....

....

....

....

....

....

13.

....

....

....

....

....

....

14.

....

....

....

....

....

....

15.

....

....

....

....

....

....

16.

....

....

....

....

....

....

17.

....

....

....

....

....

....

18.

....

....

....

....

....

....

19.

....

....

....

....

....

....

20.

....

....

....

....

....

....

'I think the world is like a great mirror, and reflects our lives just as we ourselves look upon it. Those who turn sad faces toward the world only find sadness reflected. But a smile is reflected in the same way, and cheers and brightens our hearts.'

L. FRANK BAUM
Aunt Jane's Nieces and Uncle John

AND JUST
LIKE THAT...

'Where the hell is the year going?!'

When I get together with my besties, this has become a common conversation starter. We love any excuse to hang out and eat delicious food, but it's rare to get us all together, to pin us all down. You know the score: forty-somethings juggling career goals and kids' bedtimes, cats to consider and dogs to rescue, loft extensions to build and walls to knock down. We laugh a lot. The old jokes are still fresh to us, still really tickle us. We don't believe for a second that we've changed and simply cannot fathom that the ridiculous anecdotes that we still indulge in from our university days actually happened twenty-plus years ago. On the other hand, we can't hack it like we used to. We're slower on the grape, more interested in the menu. Getting home for a good night's sleep is preferred over a sneaky nightcap, and we're not afraid to admit it. But one thing that seems to freak us out collectively is how quickly our lives are flashing before us.

'It was Christmas five minutes ago,' says one pal, 'but I don't have a free weekend until July.'

'Tell me about it,' says another. 'I gave birth to my son yesterday ... and he's turning ten on Saturday!'

A jam-packed life can be joyous, filled with gratitude to all who want to play a part in it. But it can also take my breath away. I get caught out, for a brief moment here and there, realizing that I'm going at such speed that I might arrive at whatever destination I'm heading towards a little baffled by how I got there. This scares me, and I'm not alone.

And when we pause, we tend to question rather than accept. *Am I doing the best for my kids? Should we live abroad? Do we need more space? Is the city bad? How do I accept the quiet times and thrive better when it's full-on? Will I ever make a bold decision again; ask those big questions, send that potentially life-changing email? Or am I too scared? Gosh, am I still scared of failure? Can I still have big dreams or should I let them go?*

Then, time's up! You press play and there's no time to figure out the answers. Instead of wishing on the stars and allowing that eureka moment to happen, we're too busy hanging out the washing while simultaneously answering emails. We're binge-watching *Better Call Saul*, then cursing ourselves for managing only five hours sleep a night.

Last Spring, I went to California. There's something about the blue sky on the Pacific coast. It's brighter. So much bigger. I had some headspace as we drove down the wide highways. The kids seemed content just looking out the window and trying to spot the Hollywood sign. It spurred me on to think big, think about our next step. What sort of leap, if any, was I ready to take? Whatever that might be, I should do it soon. The years are flying by so fast...

...And before we knew it, we were back home, back to the routine, back to whizzing through life and updating the diary for days, weeks, months ahead. Which is fine. It was good to be back. You can't beat your own bed, or your own hairdryer (a glimmer). But I catch a glimpse of my tired face in the

'PERHAPS WE JUST NEED TO LOOK UP, ONCE IN A WHILE, AND STARE AT WHATEVER SKY HANGS ABOVE OUR HEADS.'

mirror and wonder if the collagen supplements are working, and think, 'Wouldn't it be great to have another couple of hours in the day?' I hold my children's hands on the way to school and want to cherish their little fingers on my palm, only we're running late and hoping to make it to the gates before the bell rings. Somewhere in my head, I toy with that possible idea for a bestseller, a screenplay, then lose all track of my thoughts when the doorbell buzzes and it's an Amazon parcel, again. Another day passes.

Tomorrow will be clearer ... or maybe it never will be.

John Lennon wrote that, 'Life is what happens to you while you're busy making other plans'. It really is all the little stuff in between that counts just as much – if not more – than the dates we pin down and the meet-ups we show our faces at. Some of it is sprinkled with glimmers: that perfect cup of tea, the bedtime stories. Some of it sucks: waiting for that phone call, battles to fight. But time is completely out of our control. It's funny how we find such a solid fact so hard to accept.

Perhaps we just need to look up, once in a while, and stare at whatever sky hangs above our heads.

This is where we are. So this is where we should be.

'Happiness is not something ready-made. It comes from your own actions.'

DALAI LAMA XIV

TO GLIMMER, OR NOT TO GLIMMER

We have a choice to make. In some ways, it's much less complicated than deciding on which brand of salami to choose in the cold-meats aisle. It's more simple than any of that. Shall I choose to look for the glimmers in my life? Or not?

Sure, this can seem somewhat fanciful. You won't be alone in feeling, perhaps, cynical. Glimmers are real, though. They exist in the same way that triggers do and therefore they deserve the recognition. Manifesting glimmers can make us happier. They won't eliminate bad thoughts, but they are glowing snippets of positive energy that can combat the impulse to overthink. To be in the moment. It's about making a switch. A minute choice.

Self-love is sold to us from all platforms. While there is ample joy to be had in going for that facial, that golf weekend, that yoga retreat, these acts of pampering are a luxury not everybody can afford. We are capable of falling in love with ourselves without having to woo Number One with fancy gifts. It's possible you already have...

Think back to when you were younger. What were you *doing*? Don't put yourself under pressure to recall the best day trip or birthday party. This isn't about pin-pointing your happiest memory. Don't force a feeling that doesn't exist. Just picture yourself, sitting down, playing... What was it that warmed your heart, or made you feel safe, or made you smile from the inside out?

I am sitting cross-legged. The rug tickles my bare legs. I'm playing with my Sindy dolls, dressing them up. The little plastic shoes are hidden in the rug and every time I find a pair, satisfied, I slide them onto one of the dolls' feet. I rub the crinkled texture of a miniature ball gown between my fingertips, the red velvet hearts on a teeny skirt. I'm alone, my imagination free to soar. I can make up any story I wish, and I know it, but I'm choosing to dress the dolls, brush their tatty hair, line them up beside one another...

I am outside the shop. School doesn't start for another fifteen minutes. We always arrive a bit early so that we can hang around and chat. I've bought a chocolate bar. The boy I like is here and he's making us all laugh. I don't think I actually fancy him, like genuinely want to like, kiss him or anything. His initials are not scratched into my pencil tin. But he's so funny. I have nothing to say, but I don't care because I can't stop laughing. My friend gets off the bus and passes me a note. We've been writing letters to each other at night and exchanging them in the morning. We use teenage abbreviations on purpose, like '4eva' and 'luv'. She writes 'Hayleeee' or '2 Hailz' on the homemade envelope and I'm all for it...

I am in the library. I go to the aisle where the biographies are kept and look for books about the life of Judy Garland. I'm such a fan. To my surprise, there's a new book there, written by a different biographer. What joy. The pages are thick, yellowed. It's one of those books that has a middle section with black-and-white photographs. The paper in that section is smoother, bright white, and I run my finger across the images. As the librarian checks my card and stamps the books, I watch and daydream about having a job like that one day...

I leave the pub with a friend. Summer is at its kindest. It's gone 10 pm and there's no need for a jacket. The air so calm, so still. A few doors down, the smell of vinegar is too strong to resist. We walk through the quiet suburban streets, blowing on piping-hot chippy chips drenched in thick curry sauce, using a little wooden fork...

I am in bed, stirring, one eye peeking at the clock. Wonderful. I don't have to get up for at least another hour. My kids come in, no doubt about to demand breakfast or to be allowed to watch TV. But they don't say a word. Instead, they just clamber onto the bed and nuzzle between us, under the duvet. One of them utters a few words, and the other mutters something too. Then we doze off. All of us. A delicious morning slumber...

So you see, glimmers have always been there, right from the start. They were caught in the moment. In the ordinary. The so-called good old days – whether it was 1985, or 1993, or 2000, or 2011, or 2023 – were once just, the *days*.

Today, you might be experiencing a whole range of glimmers that one day you'll feel nostalgic about. Or, you can choose to cherish them now. Anticipate them. See them. Hold them up and allow them to shine in all their glimmering glory.

What you choose to do next *can* be a glimmer.

Breathe...

When you least expect it, oh! You'll find another.

The end.

✦

'My rainbow is faint
but it's here
the colours may not carry
the deepest hues
nor take up the whole sky
but after every rain
comes a glimmer of hope
laced in soft rose and indigo
and for me – *that is enough.*'

ALEXANDRA VINCENT
'Glimmer of Hope'

ACKNOWLEDGEMENTS

It's one thing to find glimmers. But another to collect glimmers and be directly inspired by other people at the same time. A huge thank you must go Linda Steiner, Siri Steinmo, Alexandra Vincent, Natasha Hatherall-Shawe at *Raemona*, Anthea Ayache at *The Ethicalist*, Lydia Bradley, Cheryl Castree, and Jade Kavanagh and Camilla Bolton at Darley Anderson Agency and Associates. Thank you for supporting my exploration of glimmers and for offering your glimmers in return.

I want to express my love and gratitude to my closest friends – the Lipa crew – for making glimmers easy to spot in your presence.

For your endless support, love and kindness, thank you to Oliver Sutton, and to our little glimmer-givers, Milo and Phoebe.

And of course, a big shout-out to my mum and dad, Angela and Paul, who have always pointed me in the right direction. Thank you for setting me up to find glimmers everywhere.

INDEX

Your Notes

Pavilion
An imprint of HarperCollins*Publishers* Ltd
1 London Bridge Street
London SE1 9GF

www.harpercollins.co.uk

HarperCollins*Publishers*
Macken House
39/40 Mayor Street Upper
Dublin 1
D01 C9W8
Ireland

10 9 8 7 6 5 4 3 2 1

First published in Great Britain by Pavilion
An imprint of HarperCollins*Publishers*
2024

ISBN 978-0-00-870582-4

MIX
Paper | Supporting
responsible forestry
FSC™ C007454
www.fsc.org

This book contains FSC™ certified paper
and other controlled sources to ensure
responsible forest management.

For more information visit:
www.harpercollins.co.uk/green

Publishing Director: Laura Russell
Commissioning Editor: Lucy Smith
Editor: Angela Koo
Editorial Assistant: Shamar Gunning
Designer: Lily Wilson
Production Controller: Grace O'Byrne
Layout Designer: maru studio G.K.
Proof-reader: Molly Price
Indexer: Colin Hynson

Printed and bound by PNB Print in Latvia

Poem on page 169 reproduced by kind
permission of Alexandra Vincent.